Key Stage 1

Habitats and Food Chains

by Ruth Owen

Published in 2016 by Ruby Tuesday Books Ltd.

Editor: Mark J. Sachner
Designer: Emma Randall
Consultant: Judy Wearing, PhD, BEd
Production: John Lingham

Photo credits:
Alamy: 5 (top), 10 (bottom), 21 (bottom left), 26; FLPA: 5 (bottom), 9 (top), 14 (top), 15 (left), 16, 17 (top), 17 (bottom), 23, 31 (top); Istock Photo: 27 (top); Nature Picture Library: 8 (top), 25 (centre); Photoshot: 20 (top); Science Photo Library: 19; Shutterstock: Cover, 1, 2–3, 4, 6–7, 8 (bottom), 9 (bottom), 10 (top), 11, 12–13, 14 (bottom), 15 (right), 18, 20 (bottom), 22, 24, 25 (top), 25 (bottom), 27 (bottom), 28–29, 30, 31 (bottom).

British Library Cataloguing in Publication Data (CIP) is available for this title.

ISBN 978-1-910549-79-7

Printed in Poland by L&C Printing Group

www.rubytuesdaybooks.com

Contents

Words shown in **bold** in the text are explained in the glossary.

The download button shows there are free worksheets or other resources available. Go to:
www.rubytuesdaybooks.com/scienceKS1

What Is a Habitat?

What do a garden, a woodland and a desert have in common? They are all types of habitats.

A habitat is a natural **environment** that is home to plants, animals and other livings.

Snail

The living things in a garden get what they need to live from their habitat.

Thrush

This thrush is eating snails. It smashes open a snail's shell on a patio slab!

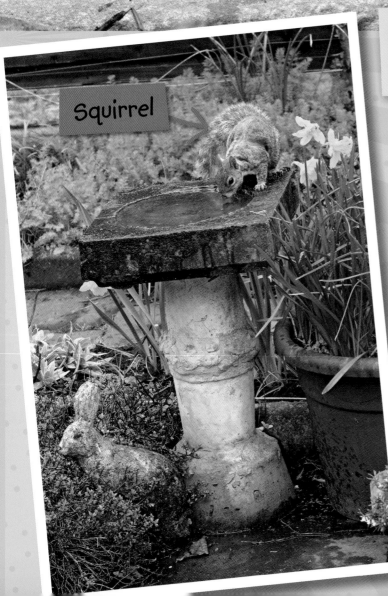

Squirrel

Let's Talk

What do you think plants and animals need from their habitat?

A Garden Habitat

You might not notice the soil in a garden, but without it the plants would have nowhere to grow.

Soil

Lettuce plants

Plants take in water and **nutrients** from soil through their roots.

Lawn

2.5 cm

A lawn isn't just one plant. In a square of lawn this big, there are up to 10 individual grass plants.

Plants make food for
energy inside their leaves.

To do this they need
air and sunshine.

 Explore!

Make a map of a garden or your
school playground.

Gather your equipment:
- Paper with 1-cm squares
- Coloured pencils
- Camera or phone

1. Begin by measuring the size of the garden
   using big steps. Using your measurements,
   draw the edges of the garden. Each step
   will be one square on the paper.

2. Now draw the garden's trees, grass and
   other plants on the map. Also add details
   such as paths, a shed or a patio.

3. Go on a wildlife treasure hunt. When you
   see a bird, snail, bee or other animal add
   a X on the map in the place where you
   spotted it.

4. Draw the animals or take a photo of them.
   You can also make a tally chart.

Where did you see the most animals?
Why do you think this is?

Did you spot an animal eating?

Did you find a nest or animal home?

Garden Homes

Beneath the lawn, ants have dug a nest in the soil.

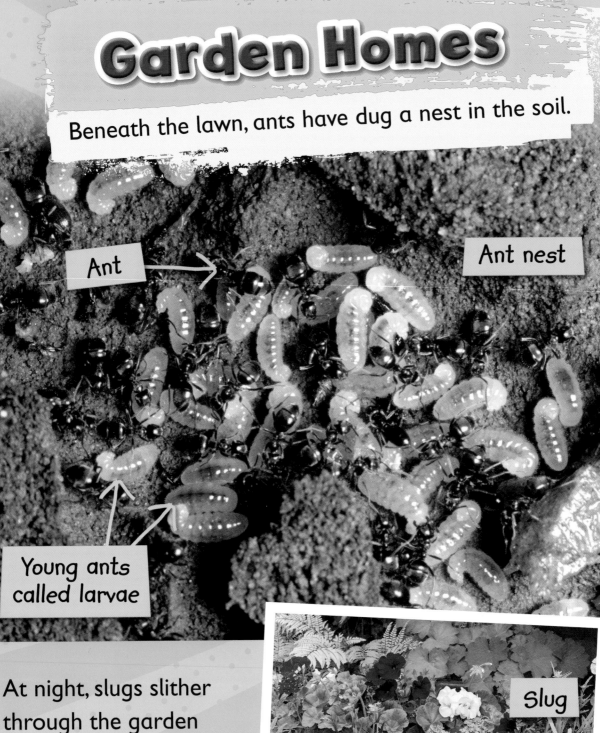

Ant

Ant nest

Young ants called larvae

At night, slugs slither through the garden eating plants.

By day, they hide in dark, damp places, such as under flowerpots.

Slug

This hedgehog has made a nest under a garden shed.

Hedgehog

The sleepy animal is returning home after a night of hunting for slugs, snails and worms.

Slug

Hedgehogs are **nocturnal** animals. This means they are active at night and they sleep during the day.

Food in a Garden

Animals in a garden get the water and food they need from their habitat.

Birds feed on insects and seeds.

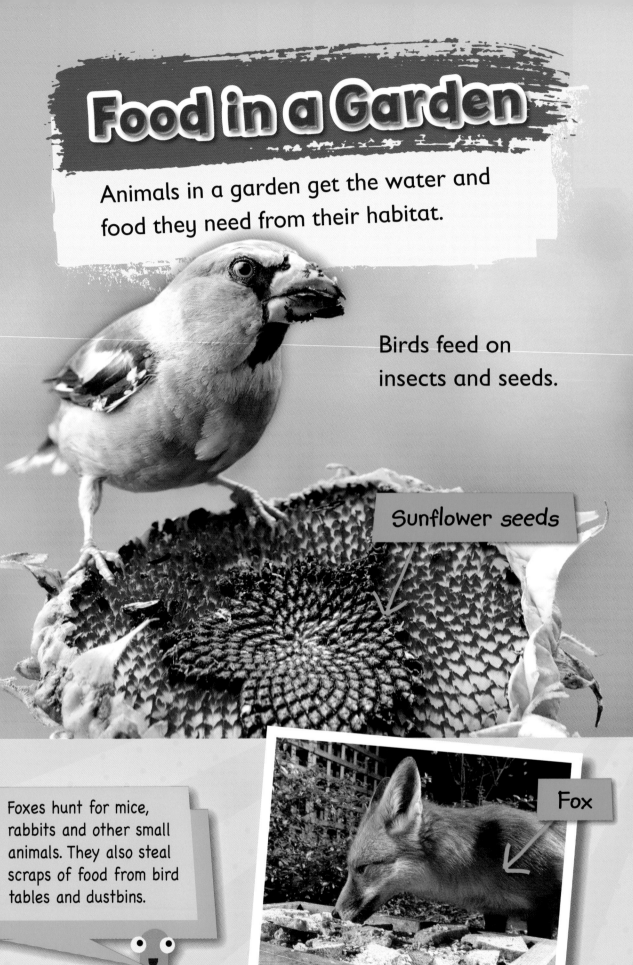

Sunflower seeds

Foxes hunt for mice, rabbits and other small animals. They also steal scraps of food from bird tables and dustbins.

Fox

What Is a Food Chain?

A food chain is a way to show what the plants and animals in a habitat eat.

This is a garden food chain.

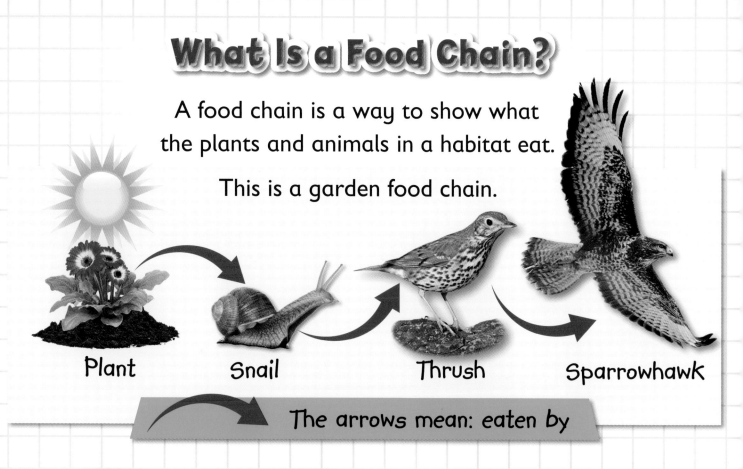

Plant   Snail   Thrush   Sparrowhawk

The arrows mean: eaten by

We say a plant is a producer because it produces its own food using sunlight.

An animal is a consumer because it eats, or consumes, plants or other animals.

Let's Draw It!

Look at these pictures.

Can you put them in the correct order to make another garden food chain?

Draw and label your food chain.

(The answer is at the bottom of the page.)

Slug   Plant   Fox   Hedgehog

Answer: Plant → Slug → Hedgehog → Fox

A Woodland Habitat

A woodland is a habitat where lots of trees grow closely together.

In a woodland you might spot these tree leaves.

Beech

Oak

Horse chestnut

A Scots pine tree has thin, needle-like leaves.

Some woodlands have deciduous trees, such as oaks and beeches, that drop their leaves in autumn.

Some woodlands have evergreen trees, such as pine trees, that have leaves all year round.

Evergreen trees

Ferns

Ferns and other small plants that like to live in damp, shady habitats grow on the woodland floor.

Who Eats Who?

In a woodland, worms feed on dead leaves that fall from trees.

Worm

Shrews, badgers, toads, birds and other woodland animals feed on worms.

Shrew

Jays search for acorns, seeds and insects to eat.

Jay

Tawny owls swoop through the trees hunting for shrews, mice, voles, rabbits and small birds.

Tawny owl

Let's Talk

How do you think an old dead tree stump is useful to a tawny owl?

Tawny owl

Shrew

Worm

Leaves

15

A Woodland Nest

A tawny owl lays her eggs in a hollow tree stump or tree hole.

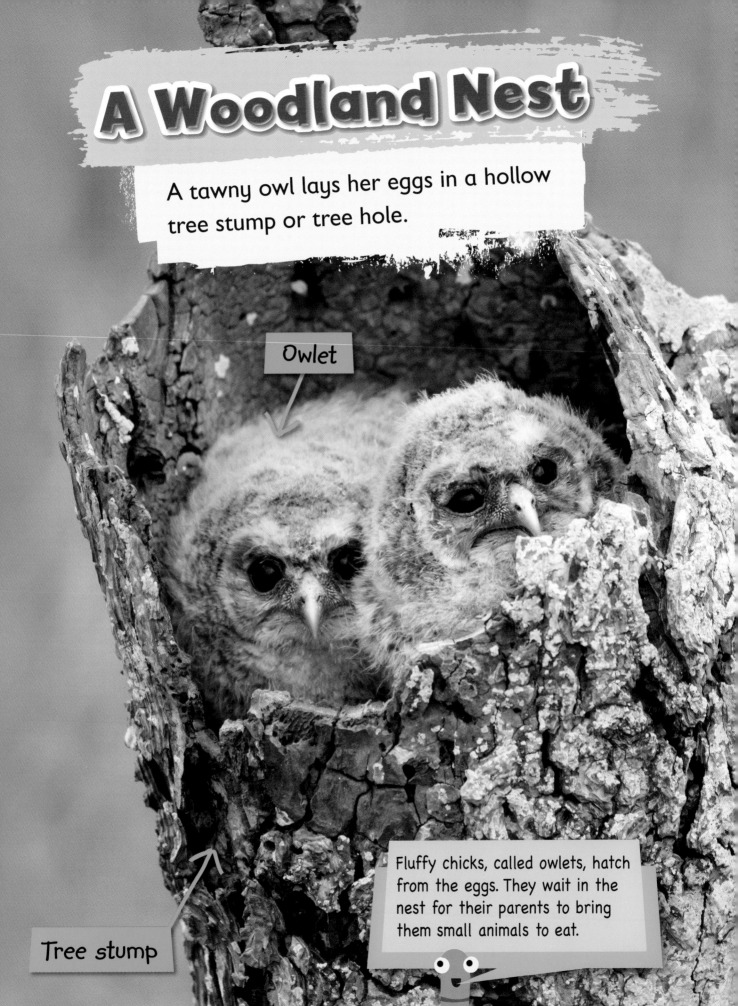

Owlet

Tree stump

Fluffy chicks, called owlets, hatch from the eggs. They wait in the nest for their parents to bring them small animals to eat.

You might spot this animal in a woodland.

What do you think it is?

What do you think it eats?

You might see this object on the ground in a woodland.

What do you think it is?

(The answers to the questions are at the bottom of the page.)

Answers: The animal is a caterpillar that will become a moth called a puss moth. Caterpillars feed on leaves. The object is an owl pellet. After an owl has swallowed an animal whole, it later spits out the bones, teeth and fur in a lump. This lump is called a pellet.

Micro-habitats

Within a large habitat there are lots of small micro-habitats.

Moss

This rotting tree stump is a micro-habitat in a woodland.

It is home to small animals and tiny plants, such as moss.

Millions of tiny animals called tardigrades may live in the moss on a tree stump.

They feed on juices from the moss.

Tardigrade

This picture of a tardigrade was taken by a **microscope**. In real life, the little animal is less than 1 mm long.

A Tree Stump Habitat

Look under a rotting log and you might see woodlice, centipedes, beetles and spiders.

Woodlouse

Centipede

Woodlice feed on dead or rotting plants. Centipedes are fast-moving hunters that feed on woodlice and small insects.

A Tree Stump Food Chain

Rotting wood   Woodlouse   Centipede   Mouse

Be a Scientist!

What type of habitat does a woodlouse prefer?

Gather your equipment:
- A small jar, spoon and paintbrush
- 12 woodlice
- A shoebox
- Cotton wool
- Water
- Pebbles
- Cling film
- A notebook and pen

1. Find about 12 woodlice by looking under logs and stones. Use the spoon and paintbrush to gently scoop and brush the woodlice into the jar. Ask an adult to help you.

2. Prepare four different habitats in the shoebox:
   - Wet cotton wool with pebbles on top
   - Dry cotton wool with pebbles on top
   - Wet cotton wool
   - Dry cotton wool

Wet cotton wool with pebbles ↘

Dry cotton wool with pebbles ↙

Woodlice habitats

Dry cotton wool

Wet cotton wool

Which corner, or habitat, do you think the woodlice will prefer? Why? Write your ideas in a notebook.

3. Gently place the woodlice in the box and cover the box with cling film.

4. Observe the woodlice to see what they do. After 30 minutes, check the four habitats.

Which habitat was most popular?

Do the results match your ideas?

What do the results tell you about woodlice?

5. Carefully return the woodlice to the place where you found them.

(There are some answers at the bottom of the page.)

Answers: The woodlice probably hid in the wet cotton wool with pebbles on top. This is because woodlice prefer to live in dark, damp habitats, such as under stones and logs.

A Rock Pool Habitat

Peek into a rock pool at the beach, and you're exploring a micro-habitat!

Rock pool

Seaweed

Green, red and brown seaweed clings to the rocks in the pool.

Seaweed looks like a plant, but it's actually **algae**. Like plants, seaweeds make their own food using sunlight.

A rock pool is home to microscopic algae and animals called **plankton**.

Just one litre of rock pool water contains millions of plankton!

Plankton

Rock Creatures

Mussels, limpets and tiny barnacles cling to the rocks that form the edge of a rock pool.

Mussels

Barnacles

Limpets

Limpet shells

Once the tide comes in, the rocks and animals are covered in seawater.

Limpets move around underwater feeding on seaweed.

Mussels and barnacles eat plankton that's floating in the water.

Trapdoors

Barnacles

Legs

Barnacle

Once it's underwater a barnacle opens two tiny trapdoors in its shell. It grabs plankton from the water with its legs.

Let's Talk

What do you think has happened to these barnacles?

Rock Pool Hunters

Rock pool **predators**, such as dog whelks and starfish, hunt for **prey** such as barnacles and mussels.

Dog whelk

Empty barnacle shells

A dog whelk makes a hole in a barnacle's shell using a hard body part called a radula.

Then the whelk feeds on the soft barnacle inside.

How Does a Starfish Eat a Mussel?

A starfish's mouth is on its underside.

Starfish

Mussel

Tiny feet pull open the mussel's shell.

The starfish pushes its own stomach out through its mouth and into the mussel's shell.

Juices from the starfish's stomach turn the mussel into a soupy meal!

A Rock Pool Food Chain

Plankton

Mussel

Starfish

Seagull

A Desert Habitat

A desert is a habitat where very little rain or snow falls.

In the Sonoran Desert the weather can be very dry and scorching hot.

Sonoran Desert in the United States

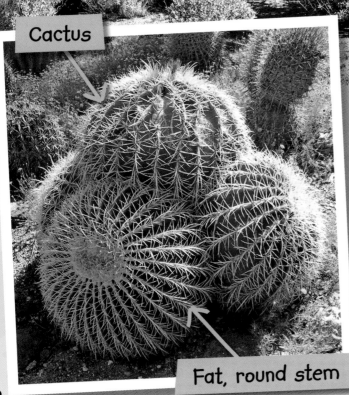

Cactus

Fat, round stem

Plants called cacti grow in this desert.

When it rains, a cactus takes in water through its roots.

It stores the water in its stems – sometimes for years!

Saguaro cactus

Birds, bats and insects feed on sweet **nectar** from a saguaro's flowers.

Most cacti have sharp spines.

Stems

A large saguaro cactus that's full of water may weigh as much as an elephant.

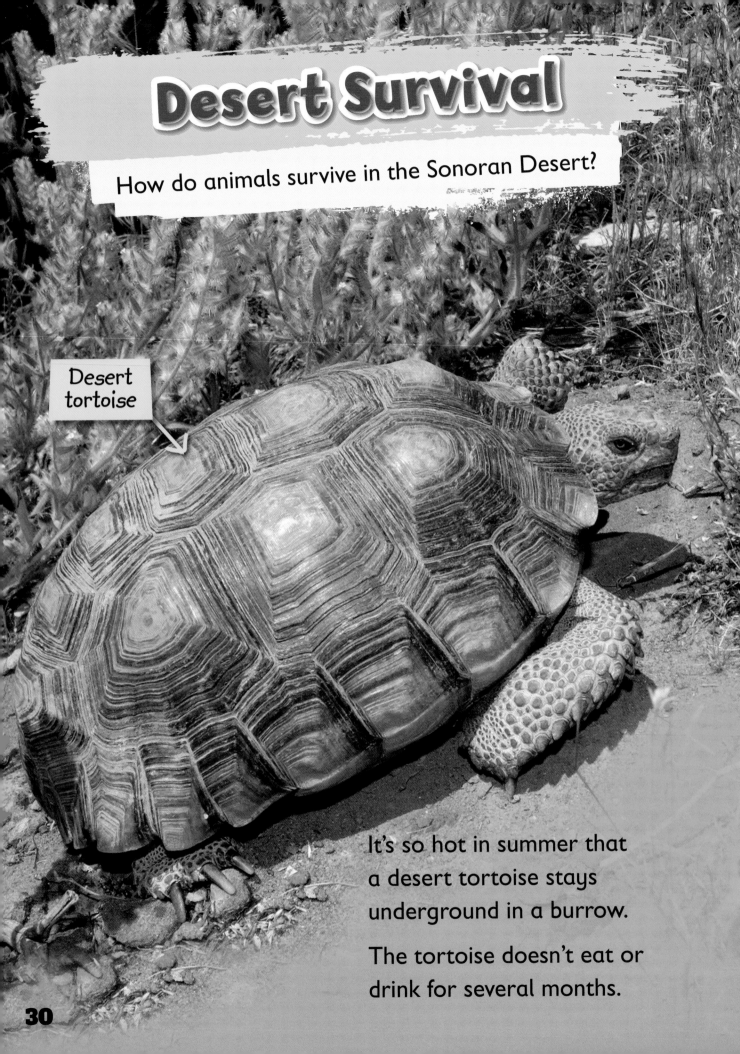

Desert Survival

How do animals survive in the Sonoran Desert?

Desert
tortoise

It's so hot in summer that
a desert tortoise stays
underground in a burrow.

The tortoise doesn't eat or
drink for several months.

During the hot day, a tiny kangaroo rat stays cool in its burrow.

At night it leaves the burrow to search for seeds, grass and leaves to eat.

To escape from predators such as rattlesnakes and bobcats, a kangaroo rat can leap 1.8 m in a single hop.

Let's Draw It!

Can you put these living things in the correct order to make a desert food chain?

Draw and label your food chain.

(The answer is at the bottom of the page.)

Kangaroo rat

Plants

Bobcat

Rattlesnake

Glossary

algae
Plant-like living things that mostly grow and live in water.

environment
The place where animals, plants and other living things make their home, and all the things, such as air, weather and soil, that affect them.

microscope
A piece of equipment used for seeing things that are too small to see with your eyes alone.

nectar
A sweet liquid made by flowers.

nocturnal
Only active at night. Nocturnal animals sleep during the day.

nutrient
A substance that a living thing needs to grow and be healthy.

plankton
Microscopic living things, such as animals and algae, that float in water.

predator
An animal that hunts and eats other animals.

prey
An animal that is hunted by other animals for food.

Index